A

(cosmic, comical, complicated)

Life

Alone

"A (cosmic, comical, complicated) Life Alone," by Carla Bastos. ISBN 978-1-62137-281-3 (Softcover) 978-1-62137-282-0 (Ebook).

Manufactured in the United States of America.

To Zendejas

Table of Contents

Introduction

I once had a conversation with a friend who was perpetually trying to get me out of the house. He was genuinely worried about me, convinced that my lifestyle was not a healthy one and, if I kept it up, I would surely be headed for total destruction.

My friend just didn't understand. There are countless people who choose to spend much of their personal life in solitude. Oftentimes these are the folks whose professional life calls for socializing and making nice with a wide variety of characters, and their work life more than fulfills any need for social

1

interaction. Their soul is at its best when immersed in that which brings it peace, and peace is its highest priority. These are the ones who feel no obligation to embrace the popular notion of a well-rounded life. In the eyes of others, there is a certain quirkiness to this group, but by their own standards theirs is the only lifestyle that makes sense. It is not selfish, unhealthy or dangerous. It is not rebellious. It is not creepy, except to casual observers whose time would be better spent getting lives of their own.

So, the day came when I had to sit my friend down and try to explain my ways and the reasoning behind them. It was not easy.

Really, what is it that makes you think I'm not happy?

It's not that I don't think you're happy. I just wonder if you're fulfilled. Without having friends in your life and getting out once in a while, it's like your life is not whole.

But, I do have friends, just not a gaggle of them. And I do get out, just not as often as you do. That doesn't mean my life is not complete. What does complete even look like, anyway? Doesn't it mean something different to everyone?

Maybe so, but something is missing when you stay in and stay to yourself as much as you do.

But, why? Shouldn't I be the one to determine if something is missing? What if I just don't need the same things in my life as you do? I am fine. I am happy. I am complete. When I don't feel so fine is when I'm forced into crowds or social events that I don't want. You know how uncomfortable that makes me.

He wasn't getting it. He was a good friend, but perhaps not the sharpest tool in the shed. He lived in a simple, one-dimensional world of noise and activity for the sake of noise and activity. He just couldn't fathom how life could be any good without at least a few evenings a week at the trendiest clubs and restaurants, constant phoning and texting, and always having a house full of company. My lifestyle included none of those activities, and I didn't miss them. Yet, my friend thought mine was the one-dimensional world.

There is another societal subset that falls into the category of loner just because they don't follow the multitudes. They may not spend the bulk of their time alone, but neither do they spend it keeping up with the Joneses or tracking the trends of pop culture. These people are loners because they are original thinkers, unaffected by what some talking head on television tells them they should be thinking or doing. They have their own brand of quiet, and it simply involves tuning out what doesn't matter to them. For them, this separation from the nonsense of the world doesn't even take much practice. It just comes naturally. They, too, are living A Life Alone.

Those who love quiet and embrace solitude, those who march to their own drumbeat and are not deterred or swayed by popular opinion, will no more convince others that theirs is a good life than others will convince them it is not. And there's a reason for that. Some of us were *designed* for this lifestyle, so it is the only lifestyle that will work for us. But for others, it cannot work. We are just wired differently.

Once I accepted that truth, I stopped trying to convince people that I was okay.

Hopefully, the proof would be in the pudding and they would see for themselves that I was not a total basket case.

But, even if they didn't, I couldn't let it concern me. I was too busy enjoying A Life Alone.

To Be or Not to Be (alone)

During a recent indulgence of my inner hermit, I found myself curled up on the living room floor, wrapped in my leopard print Snuggie (a gift from my granddaughters), eating dark chocolate-covered pretzels, sipping Merlot and reading *Team of Rivals*.

As it often did, this unplanned piece of heaven just happened. After a long day of being a suit and slogging through the requisite schmoozing and shoulder-rubbing, I wanted nothing more than to be alone. On Planet Carla, that could mean many things. Tonight it meant chocolate pretzels and wine for dinner on the living room floor. And once I knew it was happening, I went with it, totally surrendering to this wonderful massage of the senses, and allowing no one else in. Then the phone rang.

Did you ever hear your phone or doorbell ring and glare at it with disdain and suspicion, refusing to answer? You, too, might just be living A Life Alone.

Often our reactions to the world around us will reveal whether this Life is our life. We may not even know we have it in us, maybe because we think of it as a bad thing. But, it shouldn't be confused with being lonely or being an outcast. If it's a comfortable life for us, then it's easier than we may think to give ourselves license to live it.

The solo life can be a rich and colorful one, multilayered and abounding in options. This is my life, and there are many others out there who embrace it. But, there are also many who might be afraid of what it may hold. The truth is, we can't really know until we at least summon the nerve to stick our toe in the water.

I was once assured by a friend that I was not a non-conformist at all, and probably not even very different from the masses, because I held a job and took care of my responsibilities. I explained that it wasn't about any concerted effort to be different. I just felt different, not quite fitting in, and I was okay with that.

In the book *Party of One: The Loners' Manifesto,* author Anneli Rufus addresses the question of loners accepting themselves and not bothering about whether others understood them:

> *Perhaps you say "no way." You know yourself as ordinary, even dull—a wage slave with kids and taxes and a Toyota. But we will not escape the raised eyebrow, the watchful neighbors who whisper about us. "She never has anyone over!" "His bedroom light is on at the strangest hours!" Being a loner might feel natural for you. It might seem nothing, might seem normal compared to some of what is taken for granted in America: tongue piercing, for instance, or eating ground-up spleens and eyeballs cooked in casings and called hot dogs, or keeping an arsenal of automatic pistols in the living room.*

> *And yet even the dullest loners have been called eccentric just for being*

loners. Those loners might be surprised to hear it... the loner in the plain white shirt and khaki shorts eating at Taco Bell is lumped together with the odd duck who lives up a tree and talks only in iambic pentameter. We need to come to terms with this. If you are a loner, whether you sleep on a bed of nails or a queen-size Sealy Posturpedic beside your perfectly ordinary partner, chances are that someone sometime will call you eccentric. Whether you like it or not.

Sometimes my aloneness is nothing more than an hour-long lavender bath with the phone turned off and classical music or my *Wait Wait Don't Tell Me* podcast playing. Sometimes it's sitting in the corner of a crowded room or airport, writing people's thought bubbles. If you would rather observe other people and imagine what they're thinking, where they came from and where they're going, than to actually talk to them and find out, then A Life Alone may be the life for you.

As Rufus has shown, there's a societal stigma that plagues those who make this choice. People tend to treat us with kid gloves, as if we'll either melt or explode at the drop of a hat. No one really expects our relationships to work out. We're branded as selfish or snooty. At parties, if we show up at all, we're the ones usually counted on to bring the crazy.

I've long believed that one of mankind's biggest problems is that people do not really know themselves. Many are so worried about others' impressions of them that they don't take the time to figure themselves out. It is of great importance to our mental and emotional health that we know what's in us. What we want. How we actually feel, and not how someone has told us to feel. Mind you, once we embark on this exploration, what we find may not be pretty. But we must know. Only then can we understand what works for us, and rise above the judgment of those who don't get us.

While on this journey, it's worth remembering that the only one who truly gets us is the One who made us. Being convinced of this, I long ago developed an avid, passionate prayer life, and this is what ultimately helped me to know that I was okay. I was made this way, so it was okay to *be* this way.

For me, a lifelong flirtation with OCD, a passion for books and for my own thoughts, and a long, determined effort to nurture a love for self also helped to shape my choice and my comfort with this Life. The key is learning to accept, love and be comfortable with ourselves, and then simply to be ourselves—and not try to conform to whomever everyone else is. Sure, we can change anything we're not happy with, and of course we'll need to work on any creepy anti-social traits that tend to scare folks. But, for the most part, we may be surprised to learn that it's actually okay to live the Life that feeds our soul.

There are caveats, though. There are times when, even if we've accepted who we are and what works for us, there will be terror. Questions, like, *What if I'm just kidding myself? What if I wake up one day and realize this isn't what I want at all?* So, what if you do? The great thing about being free agents in a free society is that we don't have to be what doesn't work for us. I've sometimes wondered if some people just stick to a certain lifestyle because it's what they're used to or what people have come to expect of them. (Or, perhaps just out of sheer embarrassment at the thought of admitting they're not really happy that way.)

If the loner's life works for you today, there's no guarantee it will still be working for you in ten years, or even five. So, rather than overthink it, you might just consider living in the now and figuring out what your soul is in need of today. Maybe you just need a break from the madding crowd. Maybe you need time to complete a project or degree program, to consider options, or to do nothing in particular.

We grow, we change, and so do our desires and goals in life. There came a time when I was minding my own business, reveling in the freedom of middle age and beginning to inch toward my retirement years. And, very slowly, it dawned on me. That provocative question that eventually looms over everyone living this Life, quiet and respectful at first, but then loud and demanding. Do I really want to grow old alone?

I wasn't sure. I just didn't want to think about it. And whenever I did, I became nauseous (a tell-tale sign perhaps?). I had a bucket list of travel destinations, and I'd always liked traveling by myself. But it occurred to me that some of these locales would eventually become physically demanding. So, maybe I should marry a younger man to climb mountains with me and help me with my luggage? Why not just hire a valet? It was all too daunting to think about...yet.

But I Got You A Spoonrest

Have you ever noticed the insane lengths to which we will go in the desperate last gasps of a relationship? I've often wondered if these exploits are because we don't want that particular relationship to end, or because we simply don't want to be alone. Again.

After several years of blissful aloneness, navigating my way through career moves, recreational pursuits and occasional casual relationships, nurturing my soul and finding that I rather enjoyed being a hermit for a day or for months on end at my choosing, the unthinkable happened. I fell in love. Completely, hilariously, brazenly in love.

With someone other than myself. It was baptism by fire, immediate and total immersion into a world that I knew not. And it was good and it was wonderful and it worked for a few months. And it ended.

I hadn't planned to be in love in the first place, so I certainly wasn't prepared with an exit strategy. My world was no longer neat and orderly, and I had no control over it. Resolution was not to be found in cleaning my apartment, straightening pictures on the wall, or preparing a gourmet meal for myself and enjoying it naked by candlelight with Beethoven in the background and Chris Matthews silently mouthing something on the television screen. No, none of my go-to therapies for sadness and stress would work. This went way beyond all that. I was in uncharted waters here. And my reaction to it all was bizarre.

The last time we saw each other was at my place, a planned time to talk over what ailed the relationship. We chatted casually for awhile. I told him I'd been to Bed, Bath & Beyond earlier, but needed to go back. We shared a love for that store, and with his special brand of jauntiness he joked, "Oh, get something for me!"

After watching House Hunters and agreeing those chumps had chosen the wrong residence, we began The Talk. It was surreal. I don't know what the look on my face conveyed, but I'm sure I was the proverbial deer in the headlights. Thankfully, he couldn't read my thought bubbles. *Dude, have you met me? Do you really not know the extent of my awesomeness?* Apparently he didn't. And so began The Journey.

The question quickly became, what did I really want? Early in the relationship I had opened myself up and sacrificed the joys of aloneness, slowly letting him into my space. I'd been suspicious and apprehensive at first, but it hadn't taken very long to become comfortable with that sacrifice. My neurotic, orderly little world was no longer my own, and that had seemed okay at the time because he was a bit of a neurotic and a clean freak in his own right. To this day, I am amazed at how quickly I made the transition from allowing virtually no one into my space, to sharing it with a significant other. It was proof positive that, no matter how happy and settled we are in our chosen existence, we must remain open to change and growth. In my case, I wasn't sure how reliable my heart was, but I made a conscious decision to go with it. I do not regret that decision. The outcome was difficult and painful, but it grew me into a more well-rounded person than I'd been before.

But for the time being, I was faced with *how* to walk this thing out. After having made the radical leap into the relationship, did I now want my world back, all to myself, or did I want him? At that moment, the answer was him. I'd been convinced that our worlds could meld and be shared. I'd reconciled myself to the idea, and now even relished it. I wasn't ready to let it go.

The next day I did indeed return to Bed, Bath & Beyond, and I bought him a spoonrest. Why? you may ask. Did I think a gift would change things? Was I hoping it would be a final connecting thread? Was I that concerned about countertop spillage? I don't have the answers to these questions, but I know there must have been an ulterior motive, some desperate need to do *something* to control the situation. It was not to be. I never saw him again and he never got his spoonrest. I eventually took it out of its packaging, took a liking to it and kept it for myself.

The ensuing days and weeks were a blur of various versions of twelve-step programs. Alternating between denial, anger, and rolling on the floor wailing loudly (much to my own dismay and my neighbors' chagrin), I was unable to find the good stuff in the deal. I'd somehow been brainwashed into believing being alone could never again be as wonderful as being with him.

I'd been an occasional member of a loose-knit group of friends and neighbors, about ten of them, male and female, ages 30-60, all professionals, all foodies who liked to frequent new restaurants and wine tastings. I now started hanging with them on all of these outings, a feat in itself since I didn't really know how to hang and had never thought myself cool enough for hanging in any case. But knowing I could extricate myself from the group whenever claustrophobia set in and breathing became labored, I found learning the art of hanging to be a reasonable distraction from that "thing" that I wasn't ready to face. I enjoyed it and I liked the group, but I remember on at least one occasion thinking I'd rather be at the restaurant alone, observing them, concocting their thought dialogs and free to explore my own without interruption.

So, why is it that we so naturally embrace the notion of aloneness being somehow less than the best? Even after experiencing that best, our memory is short. We're afraid to go back. Or, some people over-correct and go beyond aloneness to a darker place. There is an accepted cultural bent toward "couplehood," and if a relationship ends even on the best of terms, it's treated as a titanic Greek tragedy. Even those of us who know better get sucked into the myth that life simply cannot go on without that other. We must find a distraction and fill that space, either with another other or with a group, all the while forgetting that that's not who we really are.

Contrary to popular belief, it is not a given that those who choose A Life Alone cannot have successful, rewarding relationships. All that is really needed is a partner who gets us (and, of course, we must first "get" ourselves). As in all relationships, there must be mutual compromises, but those called for from loners may be a little more difficult. The sacrifice is greater and, once we make it, it may be harder to go back and reconcile things in our chosen lifestyle if the relationship ends.

It's also important to remember that just because a relationship ends doesn't make it a fatal life failure. It doesn't mean we must determine never, ever to enter into another union. But, what if that one fails, too? So, what if it does?

After adopting a semi-social existence to help get me through the bad stuff, The Journey became fun in many ways. For the most part, I was able to find balance, and even derive some measure of joy out of the concentrated effort it took to maintain it. (If there's anything that makes a loner happy, it is planning.) Staying busy with outside activities was a good thing but had its drawbacks, one being not enough time for needed introspection. There were a few things that I still wasn't really dealing with, but there would be time for that. I was determined not to be force-fed a healing diet. That can be as difficult and destructive as not healing at all. (When a loved one dies, for example, we're always encouraged to allow ourselves to grieve at our own pace, and that pace is different for everyone.) There just isn't an instruction manual with pat answers that work in all situations.

It took a couple of months of trying to ignore the inner voice that was calling me back to my stress-free, restful, naked-by-candlelight world, but I eventually withdrew and began to exhale. It was like coming home. (Well, it WAS coming home, and staying there.) I slowly began to enjoy quiet evenings of reading again, without my thoughts wandering and doing crazy things. Eventually, it was no longer necessary to avoid the places we'd frequented together, the foods we'd enjoyed, the humor we'd shared. I didn't have to manufacture certain activities to replace others. I was able to relax. The peace was returning.

Some in the gang of ten thought I was giving up on enjoying my life, but I didn't bother trying to explain my true joy. I promised to still hang with them once in awhile, and I kept that promise, but more often when I wanted to go out I did so by myself. I was me again. This was the good stuff. The stuff that had been there all along, waiting for my return.

Whatever your takeaway from any relationship experience, be sure it is the best for YOU. Don't settle for a replacement, and don't accept whatever may work for the rest of society. For me, the moral of this story was two-fold: find the good stuff in the deal; and don't buy a spoonrest.

Ice Cream and Anger

I marched into Trader Joe's on a mission. A hellish workday had finally, mercifully ended, and I was not a happy camper. I'd invited a friend to dinner and now regretted it, but I was determined to go through with it so as not to let the workday win.

Are you a fan of monk fruit? the perky sample guy cooed. He was blocking my path and shoving tiny paper cups in my face, and I knew my only possible escape would be to clock him. *Sure,* I lied, cleverly feigning knowledge of such things. I knew wine and I knew cheese. I didn't know from monk fruit, but what the heck?

Deciding I wasn't up to this grocery shopping expedition after all, I just chose a few nosh items that could be thrown together quickly, grabbed some ice cream for dessert and headed to checkout.

"Ma'am, it's been declined. Do you have another card?"

As one who's pretty comfortable in my own skin, I don't get embarrassed easily. This was no exception, particularly since I knew I did indeed possess wealth exceeding the needed twelve dollars. No, it definitely wasn't embarrassment causing the steam that now poured from my ears.

After five minutes of resolving the Lady-do-you-have-the-money-or-are-you-a-total-deadbeat question (the card worked on the third try), I made my way to the parking lot where a sudden torrential downpour had sent shoppers scurrying. I, of course, had no umbrella. Then I fell.

I wasn't hurt, or even humiliated. I just tripped over my own feet in my rush to get to my car, went down momentarily, dropped my grocery bag, and half-crawled across the parking lot to retrieve items that were rolling away into puddles. What else could I have expected from this day?

My hair was soaked and matted to my throbbing head. My favorite Calvin Klein suit was a mess. Rainwater ran down my face, under my collar, and down my back as I climbed into the car. Narrowly avoiding the little old lady who seemed to shun headlights despite the stormy darkness (and apparently believed she was alone in the parking lot), I quietly uttered an expletive as I eyed the crowded exit lane.

When silly, nitpicky, annoying things begin to pile up, those who live A Life Alone tend to blur the lines between things and people. Stuff happens, and it may be no one's fault in particular, but we sometimes see people as the purveyors of things. So, it helps to take a step back, do a little deep breathing, and assess things before having too much interaction with others. I sat in the car for a moment and did just that. I am pretty good at recognizing when I need to sort things out a bit, and my emotions were definitely in need of sorting. There is frustration, there is weariness, there is annoyance, and there is just plain anger. My day had already run the gamut, and I became concerned that I hadn't even yet started my evening, one in which I'd be expected to be hospitable. After all, dinner had been my idea and my friend was coming at my invitation. No one had held a gun to my head. And, I never liked begging off at the last minute if I could help it, because I didn't like it when others did it to me. (I'd always told myself that extending such consideration was the sort of thing that kept me just this side of total narcissism.) I would go home, prepare a delicious meal, and be a charming host.

I trudged into my apartment, wet paper bag just about to burst, and got to work. The plan was to chill the wine, do a little prep work, then go and change before pulling the meal together. I wasn't running too late, but the fervor that went into my slicing and dicing told me the anger had not yet subsided. I'd have to work on that. I have a carefully designed prescription in place for interacting with people in a civilized, even affable, manner under trying circumstances. When frustration turns to anger, that plan usually involves ice cream, for I am of the firm belief that ice cream and anger cannot coexist, and ice cream will always gain the upper hand. I had a half-gallon of butter pecan at the ready, but didn't yet realize just how important it would become that night.

Once all was well in the kitchen, I grabbed the soaked and nearly ruined peep-toe pumps I'd kicked off at the door and made my way to the bedroom, peeling off clothing en route, toying with the notion that the day might end up on a good note after all.

In rapid succession, each of my senses kicked in, each doing its part to paint the full picture. First I heard the dripping. Then I caught a whiff of the musty dampness. *What fresh hell was this?!* I stopped short at the sight of half of my bedroom ceiling lying in huge chunks on my bed, dresser, night stand, and strewn about the floor. The carpet squished with each step, and water was still dripping from above. The slight leak whose source the maintenance guy had been trying to locate for weeks was apparently not so slight. The water had been accumulating between the floors and, with nowhere else to go, had finally crashed through. My entire bedroom was destroyed—furniture, linens, books, everything. Nothing would be salvaged, and I would never again sleep in what had been my carefully designed, perfect little retreat.

I surprised myself by not losing it. Pretty calmly, I called the maintenance guy to come and do whatever he could, the management office to advise that I'd have to move to a new unit, and my dinner guest to advise that dinner was off and, oh, by the way, I needed somewhere to crash for the night. Then I walked to the kitchen, took out the butter pecan and a spoon, and sat quietly.

By the time the maintenance guy arrived to slap a band-aid on the mess, I'd already consumed a half pint and was calmer than ever. After packing a bag to drive to my friend's house, I'd downed another half pint and become downright sedated. It never failed. Some people drank, some smoked pot, but my remedy for anger and stress was failsafe, leaving me in control of my faculties with no temptation to scream, cuss or cry.

I had a business trip coming up in two days. There would be insurance matters to consider, no doubt a battle with management for a premium unit with a view, and then packing and moving. But for the moment, I decided to pull a Scarlett O'Hara and think about it tomorrow. I was safe. I had more ice cream. Finally, thankfully, this day was over.

Bad Girlfriend

I wish I had a nickel for every time I've heard the saying, *if you want to have a good friend, you have to be a good friend.*

There is an implied assumption in that phrase that everyone wants to have a good friend. For some of us, the challenge is knowing whether we really do want to have close friends. There are great benefits, to be sure, but along with the benefits of friendship comes great responsibility. I would venture to guess there are many more folks out there who don't really want that responsibility than are willing to admit it.

Growing up, I was considered an odd duck. The things that interested other kids were not so interesting to me. But, I found it fascinating that others were so preoccupied with such nonsense and, of course, it never occurred to me how ridiculous my own interests were in their eyes. So, there was an impasse. I can't say I made a real effort to fit in with groups; in fact, I found the many cliques in school pretty distasteful. But I did like the idea of having a "best friend." Everyone had a best friend, and I wanted to know why. What were these bonds made of? Was there really such a thing as kindred spirits? Was there someone else out there who shared my thoughts and ways? I was skeptical, but I had to know.

I remember each grade in school, which years I came close to having a best friend, and which I just couldn't be so bothered. My closest friend was a girl in the fourth grade. We were nine. I guess what made us best friends was just that we arbitrarily decided to hang out together—nothing in particular in common, nothing special to talk about. We lived near each other, walked to school together, sat next to each other in class, and sat together at lunch. Period.

Then I skipped the fifth grade and the friendship was over.

There were a couple of other quasi-best friends over the years, but as I got older there always seemed to be some mutual ulterior motive. I was helping them with their homework, they were instructing me on how not to behave like a total dork. It was probably late in middle school when it occurred to me that I didn't really need this. The pros didn't outweigh the cons. Then, there came a time in early adulthood when curiosity got the better of me again and I decided to examine the whole phenomenon a bit more. During this period of ongoing self-discovery, I learned (or imagined) all sorts of cool stuff about myself. First, I was okay. The whole best friend thing was intriguing to me, but just as an observer. I didn't want it in my life, because I wasn't willing to invest the required time and effort. Second, because I was a card-carrying oddball, I was able to be a good friend without needing other people to befriend me.

To an extent, I've always liked being a friend. That is, I enjoy serving. Some would read a savior complex into this, but that's not it. For example, I love preparing a great meal and watching people enjoy it. (I'm usually anxious for them to go home as soon as they're done, but that's another story.) I also enjoy encouraging people, largely because of what I see as a lack-of-self-esteem epidemic. But, when it comes to committing, I have issues.

It wasn't just that friendships were difficult for me. Until I'd nearly reached middle age, they just always seemed calculated. I didn't feel this was fair to the prospective friend, even if they didn't realize they were part of a strategy. This really became a problem in workplace friendships, and it took years for me to stop over-thinking things and just let friendships happen or not. But, even once I arrived at that comfort zone, I was still a stickler for boundaries. No one was allowed past the line that marked my personal space. And little by little, that line moved farther and farther out. Somehow, I needed more and more space, and there was a very real concern that that need would eventually involve entire city blocks.

During those years of working on friendships that weren't for my selfish gain, I wasn't yet sure how I felt about those who were into me for similar selfish motives. Their motives weren't any worse than my own, so I guess it was only fair. Weirdly, people always seemed to come to me for counsel. Personal relationships, professional decisions, you name it, it seemed that folks were under the mistaken notion that I had it all together and I had nuggets of wisdom to go around. Maybe it had something to do with my academic background, maybe because I was into prayer, I'm not sure, but I became the voice of reason for many. (Scary, I know.) There was a dichotomy here, because even though I sometimes felt taken advantage of, I loved helping people reach a logical conclusion to matters. And, talking with people through their issues allowed for personal interaction without commitment. Still, no one seemed interested in my issues. Or, perhaps they just didn't think I had any.

So, I decided that my inner conflict was three-fold: resentment toward those who were into me for selfish reasons; resentment toward those who didn't know or care that I had problems of my own; and, the terror that someone actually *would* care and would want to enter my world and share in those problems. As I worked through the mess, and as with so many other messes, I grew. Becoming comfortable with who you are will never happen overnight, and never without tremendous effort and at least a few bouts of tug-of-war. After long considering myself a bad girlfriend because there was no one on this earth with whom I wanted to have a sleep-over, do karaoke, or go shoe-shopping, I finally came to terms with it all.

Hopefully, at a certain point in adulthood (say, before you reach retirement), the loner in you can make peace with such contradictions. It's no fun going through life not playing well with others, and it is what drives many people past A Life Alone to an unhealthy place. To get victory over the conflict, you must first give yourself an honest answer: *Do I really want to have close friends in my life?* It's okay if you don't, but if you do, then you must decide just how close, and on what terms. And, of course, those friends must agree to those terms.

I am fortunate to have a very small number of close friends (two) who get me. They respect my boundaries and they never call me crazy, at least not to my face. They understand that I sometimes feel guilty about hijacking a conversation and making it all about me, because there are so few people I'm willing to talk to that I really need to vent when I'm with them. They know that I love them, even though I'll not show up at gatherings or events for months at a time, and when I do I have to sit with my back to the wall. They don't mind that I am me. They give me grace. And that's one of the things I love about them.

Adjustments

Age 32 was a great time. It wasn't the kind of great where life was a cakewalk, but empowerment counts for a lot, and I fclt empowered. My husband and I had successful careers and a nice home. My son did well in school, and I had the freedom to indulge my need for periodic seclusion. The marriage was okay. Not excellent, but not terrible, either. Those were the-days-of-learning-to-be-me. The grown-up me, aware but not overly concerned with the rest of the world, just raising my family and growing professionally and minding my business. Life was good. And, one day, it wasn't.

My husband died suddenly and I was thrust into the rare status of widowhood at the age of 32. The life scenes that would play out over the next couple of years were epic. It seemed every week there was a strange new hoop through which I must jump, an unfamiliar circumstance to which I must adapt. Loners don't adapt easily. We are creatures of habit, and don't like our apple carts upset. Some of those days, I felt like a toddler learning to walk; others like a paralytic who would never walk again.

In ensuing years, I learned volumes from other widows and widowers about how different personality types must each adjust according to their own need and circumstance. But, at the time, I had no frame of reference. I was living every day on a highwire over the Grand Canyon, after having overslept and missed the tightrope-walking class. I once heard Nick Wallenda talk about the adjustments he had to make to various weather conditions while on the highwire. Well, I didn't know how to make such adjustments, and in the days and weeks and months over the Grand Canyon, the sun burned my skin mercilessly, the sand blew into my eyes and blinded me, and dry air caught in my throat and made it hard to breathe. I was feeling my way through life. At six thousand feet. Without a net.

One of the oddest things to me was the new state of not fitting in. I'd never fit in, so why should this be any different? But, now it wasn't enough to just not fit in with my own peers. I had to adjust to not fitting in with whole new groups. All the other widows were in their 70s, and in those days it seemed all the other single people were 21. And, it suddenly occurred to me that all of our friends had been couple friends—I was now a fifth wheel. It was going to be interesting to see where I would land in all this (maybe not the best phrasing at six thousand feet).

My greatest takeaway from those years is a simple one, really. Life is going to keep happening until it stops. Period. Whether you like what's happening or not, and no matter how you react to what's happening, it's going to happen. Sometimes good stuff, sometimes bad. And, we even get choices in the deal. We get to decide *how* we are going to react, and that makes all the difference. We can just check out and refuse to cope (a very tempting option for loners), or we can keep putting one foot in front of the other and moving forward, even if we're on a highwire.

Grudgingly, I count those learning experiences some of the richest of my life. I watched my son Damon come of age, I balanced career, finances and household maintenance, and I was forced to interact with all sorts of people that I considered an assault on my private world. But, I grew and I adjusted. The couple friends were no longer a factor, and the loner in me was nurtured. By the time Damon finished high school and went off to college, I'd made it safely across the Canyon and felt ready for the next adjustment. It would be a radical one.

The decision to sell my home and walk away from my career didn't come easily. I wasn't exactly a young student trying to find myself. But, wanderlust consumed me, fearlessness compelled me, and I was an empty-nester who could actually do something about it.

When the opportunity to join a humanitarian mission aboard a mercy ship presented itself, I was ready. I'd always loved the notion of legitimate humanitarian work with legitimate motives, and I wanted to see the world. It was just weird enough to suit me. Family and friends thought the idea was only slightly crazier than they already thought I was, so it wouldn't be too much of a stretch. There would be an initial two-year commitment, and part of the deal— the only part that gave me pause—was that, should I die, I had to agree to be buried at sea. (Although I thought it a little far-fetched that something like that would ever happen, there came a time when a crew member succumbed to cerebral malaria and did indeed have to be buried at sea—a scene I will never forget as long as I live.)

While I had no precedent to prepare for life at sea, I was thoroughly impressed with myself and my ability to adapt. For me, the greatest adjustment was sharing the tiny bathroom facilities with so many other crew members. The greatest joy was experiencing the many countries in which the vessel would dock for weeks at a time. The work was hard, but nothing could compare to the "play," when we'd drop anchor and swim in the ocean with dolphins and whatever else happened by (that is, until the lookout spotted sharks and we'd make haste to scurry back up the rope ladder). While I couldn't feed my inner hermit as I would have liked during those years, I made up for it with long, pre-dawn sessions of prayer and meditation out on deck, watching the sun rise over a silent, glassy sea or waves rolling under a dark, threatening sky. It was a world I'd craved my entire life.

The resilience and fortitude gained during those years aboard ship would help sustain me throughout my second term of missionary work, spent on the ground in the southwest African country of Angola. A country of great beauty marred by a violent civil war and a corrupt government, Angola offered up a life that required adjustments I was unable to make. I toughed it out, getting my fulfillment by pouring myself into the work, and my balance by writing for the Associated Press and for various embassies. But, after successfully sacrificing any notion of ever having solitude again, and overcoming several bouts with malaria, and dodging and fleeing rebel attacks, Angola finally took me down with typhoid fever just a few years later. Carla's Big Adventure was about to come to a close, and I would settle back in the States just in time for September 11, 2001.

Adjusting to life in my home country may have been the greatest challenge of all. With my newly acquired global perspective, I wondered if in fact this was home. Pastimes and priorities had changed. *People* had changed, radically. Technology had taken over, and no one talked or read or wrote. Refusing to cope with any of it, I curled up into a virtual ball and began liberally feeding my inner loner, reviving her from hibernation and allowing her to have her way. I accepted my new lot as small-town newspaper editor in the already almost-dead business of print journalism, but simultaneously immersed myself in a secret world of planning my retirement.

It would either be in the southwest U.S. or in some remote corner of some unheard-of foreign country. I would become the wine connoisseur I'd always fancied myself to be. I would learn two or three more languages. I would read until I was cross-eyed and write until I dropped. I would travel at will, and my bucket list would be endless. I would never, ever again be a slave to any society. (Yes, retirement was still 20 years off, but that little detail was of no consequence to me. Why wait until the last minute to prepare?)

Making retirement plans, becoming a hermit in the truest sense of the word, and welcoming my granddaughters into the world were the next ten years of my life. It was then that the loner took on a life of her own and this Life Alone began to take shape.

Damn You, Virginia!
(the sunglasses incident)

I never wanted to move to Virginia. Having lived all over the country, on a ship and even on another continent, I'd years ago decided that the American southwest was my place. I loved the desert, but in particular I loved New Mexico. Unable to wait until retirement, I had settled there with no intention of ever leaving. Ever.

The job offer was tempting, but moreover I felt a weird, inexplicable pull to Virginia. Having prayed long and hard for wisdom and direction, I was certain there was *something,* some reason that I was supposed to make the move. I didn't understand it, but the notion that there just might be something there for me, something that might be missing and might enrich my life in some way, was just too tempting to pass up. And, of course, I was fearless, as usual paying little or no attention to the naysayers who were always telling me I shouldn't travel to foreign places alone, I shouldn't walk home from a restaurant or back to my hotel from the metro alone, blah, blah, blah.

The best/worst thing about making such life-changing decisions alone is that they are yours. You own them. The challenge, the recklessness and folly, and their consequences and rewards, belong to you, and you alone must live with them.

The decision was made and I embarked on what would be yet another extraordinary journey. But, within weeks of relocating, I knew pretty definitively that I did not belong in Virginia. I'd made a mistake. This was not my place—fine for some, no doubt, but not for me. Sometimes there are no words to say just why a thing is not for you, but at a certain point you just know. I knew. That is, I knew the place was not for me, but I thought the romantic relationship I had entered into was. I became convinced it was the real reason I'd made the move, and it made everything else tolerable. I was as happy as a little crazy clam, not allowing the dreary weather and congested traffic to put a damper on the fairy tale.

Of course, when the relationship ended, there was more traffic and precipitation than ever, as if to punish me for ignoring it in the first place. Those were the-days-of-rolling-on-the-floor-wailing-loudly. And driving in the car with tears flowing. And flooding my eyes with Visine before going into meetings. I was in a hinterland, not quite plugged in to my life, but drifting somewhere in the vicinity.

The whole crying thing was a nonsensical exercise, really, but it was my catharsis of choice. I enjoyed it. While at work, I would close my office door, turn down the lights, and revel in my daily (sometimes hourly) cleansing. It was a blast. After a while, I wasn't sure if I was crying because of the break-up, because I was stuck in Virginia, or because it just felt good.

Soon, I was enjoying it so much that I decided to buy the biggest, darkest pair of sunglasses I could find, not only to hide my ridiculousness from the rest of the world, but to look the part. (What part, I do not know, but I liked the look.)

I wore my new sunglasses everywhere, even when I wasn't bawling. I put them on before leaving the house and wore them in the elevator and on the stairs. I wore them in stores. Would I not have been fired, I'd have worn them during my workday.

As Virginia is wont to do, she poured rain on me incessantly during the-days-of-rolling-on-the-floor-wailing-loudly. I wasn't sure if it was raining on anyone else, but mine was an ugly, wet world of bad hair days and inside-out umbrellas. On occasion she would tease me with the hint of a bright sky or an almost-positive forecast, but the rains always returned in short order. The skies stayed dark, and the days stayed short. And I wore my sunglasses, anonymous and content, existing in my secret world of heartache and joy.

Ironically, even though I was embracing my misery, I still made a pointed effort to stay physically and emotionally healthy (I know—too late for that second one). I always left the office on my lunch hour, even if I didn't have a lunch date or errands to run. It was therapy. Donning my trench coat and dark glasses, I ventured out one Tuesday to see what was new at TJ Maxx, and then maybe pick up a cappuccino. It was dark at 12:30 in the afternoon, and gusty winds blew the rain horizontal. Why were all these people out for lunch on such a soggy day? Didn't they know I was out here and needed my space?

Not finding a blouse or scarf that suited my fancy, I settled for a collection of lavender sachets. There was always *something* at TJ Maxx that would feed my soul. Clutching my fragrant find as I emerged from the store, hopping over puddles all the way to my car (four-inch heels and all), I was pretty content. I wasn't crying, didn't feel happy or sad. I just felt right. And because I felt right, it never occurred to me to take off the glasses. I looked left, then right, but failed to look left again. By the time I caught the silver Mercedes in the corner of my eye, it was too late. The thick frame on my sunglasses was blocking my peripheral vision.

Thankfully, I had the presence of mind to snatch the glasses from my face immediately after the cars made contact. I knew the other driver couldn't see me in the blustery darkness, so no one would be any the wiser and I wouldn't have to explain why I was wearing them at all. But the fender bender would still be my responsibility. I checked out the minimal damage to the man's car and, at his invitation, settled into his passenger seat to exchange information. He seemed reasonable enough, even empathetic. No doubt he saw me as a normal businesswoman in a hurry, and not a heartbroken loner on the edge, wearing giant dark glasses on the stormiest day of the year.

The hardest part about the whole incident was the offense, that notion that I'd been deliberately wounded. But who had wounded me? I decided it was Virginia's fault. She had seen fit to drown me in her driving rains and envelope me in black skies. She'd broken my heart and made me cry, then twisted her miserable knife by denying me the hope of ever seeing sunshine again. Yes, surely Virginia would be found liable and I could go on wearing my dark glasses without guilt or worry.

That evening it was decided. I would have to leave. I could no longer tolerate her. I'd given her a fair chance, but I refused to accommodate her cruelty any longer. I made phone calls, talked to friends and colleagues back in New Mexico, and began planning my escape. I would go home. It would be quick and efficient. I would leave the wet darkness behind for once and for all, and head back to the sunny skies and clean, dry air of my desert place.

So, was I running away from my problems? Yes, I was. For, if it is the necessary remedy, and a doable one that won't hurt another, a loner gets to do that. So, run if you must. Or stay. But, if no one but you will be affected by your choices, then it's not rocket science. Those choices must be the ones that are best for you.

Somewhere deep down, the cruel, unrelenting Virginia must have finally come to understand the havoc she'd wreaked in my life. She'd never shown herself to care, but even she must have had a moment of compassion and realized, *This woman has had enough.* Or, maybe she just knew tormenting me was a lost cause since I'd decided to leave her. For, on the next day, when I awoke to an internal debate on the merits of staying in bed, I noticed something odd. It was warm and shiny, making its bold statement on my bedroom walls: *I am still here.* My friend, the sun.

Heading for the door that new morning, I actually hummed. And there was a lilt in my step as I grabbed briefcase, keys—and sunglasses.

Your Mama

In the terror/delight of my aloneness, I always loved/hated living on opposite coasts from my family. Not having very close family relationships anyway, I was able to avoid most uncomfortable encounters, but still enjoy those occasional long phone conversations with siblings. And I was only a short flight away from my darling granddaughters, so I had the best of both worlds.

When, after years of living sans serious romantic relationship I finally entered into one, I was gripped by an interesting phenomenon. He was a family man. A true family man who had moved back to his home state to take care of his mother, after more than 30 years away. His best friends were his siblings, and several of our dates were events that included his family. Our third or fourth date was a black tie event and, because he had to be at the venue early, my services were enlisted to pick up his mom. There was a hurricane that night, blinding rain, we got lost, couldn't find the designated parking, and arrived very late with serious hair issues. We bonded.

Even as I wondered if all of our dates were going to include his mom, I couldn't deny that I was falling in love with her. Just as I would eventually fall in love with his sister, brother-in-law and cousins.

What was it about this family that made me feel so comfortable, so much a part of them? Was it them, or was it just the notion of a close-knit family— something I'd never experienced. They were no doubt as dysfunctional as the next clan, but completely supportive of one another within their dysfunction. They had each other's back. It was amazing to see, and I vacillated between the joy of embracing them and the regret of never having experienced that joy before now.

The advantage of being a member of one of these families while living A Life Alone is that they are your social outlet, and you already know them. When it's time to get out of the house and interact with others, you don't have to worry about meeting someone new or the discomforts of forced or contrived conversation. And then you can go home. Or send them home. Your ready-made social fix, without even having to think about it.

Not that family relationships are easy by any stretch. In some ways, they require even more work, because of the greater commitment. You just can't get rid of these people. If friendships with them don't work out, there's still that whole blood thing. But, I still contend that choosing family as your social network is preferable to cultivating relationships with strangers. Too often, non-blood relationships don't end well. In most cases, the strangers live on after the bond is broken. You avoid them, you run into them, you try to be civil, but sometimes you just wish you'd never befriended them in the first place.

As my bond with my friend's family unfolded, so too did the realization that the relationship with him would not last.

As hard as that was, there was another sad proposition to consider. When we decided to go our separate ways, the unspoken, panicked cry of my heart was, "But what about your Mama?" She was my friend. I'd picked her up for church, I'd gleaned wisdom and history and humor from her, I'd loved hearing her stories. This woman's rich, multi-faceted life had become a point of intrigue for me, and I'd looked forward to our relationship growing. All of that would now be lost.

I also lamented the loss of a just-begun friendship with his sister, who shared my independent views and love for travel, who was a loner and a thinker in her own right. She was one of only two people I knew, besides myself, who had a desire to travel to Patagonia. But, she and I wanted to do it en route to Antarctica. I recalled our excitement as she and I talked about the region during Christmas dinner and discovered our shared passion. I'd actually toyed with the notion of making the trip with her and not alone.

Knowing and bonding with this family meant growth for me, on many levels. All of that would now be lost.

Such loss is the nature of the beast. No matter if you're a hermit, a loner, an introvert, or simply one who has chosen to live A Life Alone to any degree, save for the most extreme cases there must be interaction with others. We can limit it to occasional coffees, dates or dinners, and we can choose the comfort of family over strangers (along with the family gatherings that come with that package). Either way, we should be mindful that even limited interaction involves some measure of commitment, and with that will come risk. In the bigger picture of life, anything that involves commitment comes with risk, be it a career change or joining a new health club. And no condition of aloneness allows us to completely avoid that commitment.

There is some consolation in all this, maybe even some degree of control for those of us who need it. The loss we risk, the void left by the family member or loved one who is no longer there, is much harder to take than bumping into an annoying ex-friend on the street now and then. So, we get to choose into which we will invest our time and our heart. We must choose wisely, but it is our choice. And, if we're willing to take the risk, our very own families may yield a gold mine of social interaction, shared history, and comfortable humor that will greatly enhance the loner's life we have chosen.

Among Things To Ponder:
The Uniboob

When living a loner's life, all things eventually point to the number one. Including your breasts. During an installment of my post-relationship-find-a-distraction-any-distraction-at-all-costs ritual, I considered this truth in its profundity.

Sports bras are wonderful things for the health and long-term perkiness of your breasts. Racer-backs provide an amazing lift and bare shoulders for your halters and evening gowns. But at what cost? I have yet to find a sports bra or racer back that can overcome the dreaded uniboob—that pushed-together look that makes us appear to have one boob rather than two.

It's a non-issue, really, because we've all come to accept the uniboob as an unavoidable, necessary evil if we're to prevent flopping and wobbling through our workouts. But what if you just want to go to work and haven't done laundry and don't have as extensive a bra wardrobe as you should because you're perpetually broke, and all that's left in your lingerie drawer are a sports bra and a couple of racer backs? Then you're going to work with a uniboob.

(Granted, there are more important considerations in life. But, these issues matter too, and someone must ponder them.)

It's a well-settled truth that in most things, two are better than one. Our breasts are no exception. Functionally, aesthetically, and in the interest of pure symmetry, two breasts are preferred. There is a certain lostness that the uniboob endures without a significant other. It just wasn't designed to be one. But, is it an accurate microcosm of the Life Alone?

The whole two-are-better-than-one premise, from its biblical origins, was all about people, not breasts. The divine design also included a diverse range of emotional and psychological traits. As I've said, there may be many more people with the aloneness bent than are willing, or who dare, to admit it. We've bought into the idea that it's just not natural, and so we perch ourselves into one bra cup or onto a bicycle built for two, and wait for our other to come along and bring balance to our world.

Of course, many folks who choose aloneness still have significant others, and even marry. These are the wise and patient ones, those who know that they can only make it work with others of a certain ilk, and those others are few and far between. They know that they must wait for that partner who can understand, or at very least, be willing to indulge, this unique lifestyle. This brings a level of maturity to the relationship that may just be lacking in other unions. But, as in all relationships, it's important for our partner to know that our need for aloneness is not just an occasional quirk. It is what we are made of. It is who we are and maybe always will be.

Just as our breasts are an illustration of how strategic and efficient our Maker was in designing us, we must employ strategy in adopting our lifestyle. From a practical standpoint, there are some things that just can't be done alone. Who will hold the bookcase steady while you screw in the shelves? Who will pick up the FedEx package while you're out of town? Who will face the world and jump through its bureaucratic hoops when you just can't (or won't)? This is where strategic planning comes in.

There are elements of society in which we must remain engaged, like it or not. If you don't have a significant other and you're too busy writing thought bubbles to be concerned with the cares of life, then you must be willing to hire someone to do it for you. Or, maybe reach an agreement with a trusted platonic acquaintance. However you address the issue, it must be addressed and not ignored, lest you become a hoarder and a deadbeat with unpaid bills and four-inch dirty fingernails. Rather than enjoying A Life Alone, you'll be spending your days hiding from the people who want to take you away and bulldoze your apartment.

No, the most gratifying aspect of aloneness is not that we get to be lazy, unkempt slugs who ignore our responsibilities. Just the opposite. Fulfillment is found in what we can accomplish when we have order in our lives, and our thoughts are clear and uninterrupted.

In the book *Quiet: The Power of Introverts in a World That Can't Stop Talking,* author Susan Cain shows introverts to be innovative and creative. Cain says it is to introverts that we owe many of the great contributions to society—from van Gogh's sunflowers to the invention of the personal computer. She further offers:

Introverts feel "just right" with less stimulation, as when they sip wine with a close friend, solve a crossword puzzle, or read a book. Extroverts enjoy the extra bang that comes from activities like meeting new people, skiing slippery slopes, and cranking up the stereo. "Other people are very arousing," says the personality psychologist David Winter, explaining why your typical introvert would rather spend her vacation reading on the beach than partying on a cruise ship. A hundred people are very stimulating compared to a hundred books or a hundred grains of sand."

Many psychologists would also agree that introverts and extroverts work differently. Extroverts tend to tackle assignments quickly. They make fast (sometimes rash) decisions, and are comfortable multitasking and risk-taking. They enjoy "the thrill of the chase" for rewards like money and status.

Introverts often work more slowly and deliberately. They like to focus on one task at a time and can have mighty powers of concentration. They're relatively immune to the lures of wealth and fame.

Aloneness is a choice made by those of us who not only may accomplish more when we're alone, but are just plain happier that way. But, it's a good idea to do some periodic self-assessment to be sure it is indeed the lifestyle we want and from which we are deriving happiness and gratification in what we're accomplishing. In some cases, that may mean telecommuting in order to be productive professionally but in an environment that breeds creativity; in others, collaboration is necessary but within certain parameters. Sadly, some who choose a loner's existence just stop there. They don't go the extra mile to think through their decision, determine their must-haves and must-avoids, and plan out exactly what that existence should look like. But, if we don't take those strategic steps, the choice may not work for us.

The comfort and peace to be found in this Life are well worth taking a few practical steps to preserve it, so we would do well to plan ahead in order to make it work. Oh, and maybe buy a few more bras.

Just an Oil Change, Please

It's a common query. Does spending more time alone make you more or less shrewd? More or less intuitive? More or less trusting of others?

Most people's answers are subjective and self-serving. I like to tell myself that I'm a smarter, more well-rounded person because of my life choices. But then, there's the thin line between shrewdness and paranoia upon which loners are often perched, sometimes falling off to this side, sometimes to that. It's a tough call for us, because others often judge us as paranoid anyway, and we sometimes allow ourselves to be influenced by their judgment. I once spent a dizzying day stumbling between trust and paranoia, with that ever-elusive balance escaping my clutches at every turn.

Having spent several years living alone, I was used to taking care of routine home and car maintenance and, after also living in the same city for a number of years, I'd become comfortable with certain service establishments. My local Honda dealership was not one of them. Each time I went in for an oil change, tire rotation or any other minor adjustment, I was presented with a laundry list of desperately needed services and accessories. (Would life as I knew it really come to a screeching halt without a new floor mat? Seriously?) It only took a couple of visits to convince me they didn't have my best interest at heart, so my next couple of oil changes were done at local discount establishments. Unhappy with them too, I eventually went skulking back to the dealership, coupons in hand, determined to simply ignore their ploys to relieve me of my money.

In the 21st century, one would think the old car-dealers-trying-to-take-advantage-of-single-women phenomenon would be pretty much played out. Out of necessity, most of us are pretty savvy. But, sadly, it seems we are still targets of unscrupulous retailers of cars, furniture, tools, electronics and more. Long ago, in a land not so far away, male retailers were taught that women were ignorant, incapable of making a wise decision, and (apparently) walked around with money to burn. And, even after they joined the rest of us in the real world, many refused to change their tactics.

I had two errands that morning. The first stop was a certain furniture store, a big chain having a big sale. I'd been planning the purchase of new occasional chairs for a while, and today was the day I wanted to start shopping around. I tried to be invisible as I entered the store, wearing the practiced expression that I hoped conveyed it all: *I'm just looking, don't bother me, I'll call you when I need you.* It didn't work.

The man who rushed me before I'd gotten both feet inside the door was maybe in his mid-60s, no doubt someone who'd been in that first class of Female-Hating-Retailers 101. He immediately assured me he was there to help me. I politely assured him I didn't need his help. He said he could show me their just-arrived line of whatever. I ran, making my way to the other side of the store. Surprisingly spry, he stayed hot on my heels, making clear that age would not be to my advantage that day. I relented, finally considering that if I took the chance of trusting him, and put up with his nonsense for just a few moments, maybe I really could get a good deal. I stopped, turned to him with all the charm I could muster, and gave him a list of all the things I did not want. That didn't work either, as he continued trying to force-feed me his own brand of "help."

It was no use. I wouldn't be buying chairs, or anything else from this guy. After similar experiences at two more furniture stores, I finally did find what I wanted, made the purchase and delivery arrangements, and ran for the door. I still had another errand to tackle.

I just needed an oil change. Nothing more. Although six years old, my car had only 40,000 miles on it and was in great condition. Now living in a new city and wanting to avoid the local dealership, I'd gotten a few references, checked out some reviews online and made a list, finally settling on what appeared to be a reputable establishment. Things seemed okay at first—clean environment, friendly but businesslike staff. But, within moments of my car going up on the lift, a worried-looking mechanic made his way to the corner where I sat rolling my eyes behind my dark glasses. *Ma'am, I'm afraid your battery's about to go. Have you noticed you're not getting much power?* I scowled. Should I make the quick decision to trust the guy and bite the bullet for a new battery, or take my chances that he, too, was lying to me? I decided to get another opinion. *No, just do the oil change for right now.*

The look on his face was a sure sign that either he wasn't lying after all, or that he was a great actor.

Retrieving my checklist from my pocketbook, I decided to make an appointment with the second runner up—but I would wait until tomorrow. I was already tired of dealing with these clowns. After paying for the oil change, I began driving back over the hill toward home. The car hesitated. It felt as if it just didn't want to go. I hadn't noticed this before, and immediately thought something had been done to my car. I slowly made my way to the runner-up, knowing I'd probably have to be there the rest of the day without an appointment.

Wow, you got here just in time, the grease-covered young man muttered once he'd taken a look. *It's your battery.*

He even showed me the corrosion that had been spreading for a while (and not just inflicted moments earlier). He was all business, very matter-of-fact. Sufficiently shaken up, I instructed him to install the new battery right away. I even asked if he'd noticed anything else I should be aware of. This guy was suddenly my new best friend, whose only concern was my safety and comfort. (Amazing how little it took for me to come to that conclusion!)

I'd been planning to drive on the interstate to a friend's home later that evening. This could have been bad. Really bad. Not that getting a second opinion was wrong, but my trusted intuition was now in question. Had I become so jaded that I just didn't trust *anyone* anymore? Had I been burned so many times by so many people that it was an automatic reaction, a survival mechanism of sorts?

Interestingly, when I thought about it, I *hadn't* been burned that often. A few times, sure, but never was it because my guard was down or I was just naïve. Sometimes it just happens, but it is unfair to the population at large to assume everyone is lying every time. Besides, in the grand scheme of things, I had relatively little money to steal anyway. I probably didn't make a very good target.

I'm still not sure if a lesson was learned that day. My momentary trust of the first furniture guy hadn't gotten me what I wanted. And, my distrust of the auto mechanic hadn't prevented the worst from happening. In fact, it almost *caused* the worst to happen. So much for shrewdness. Guess I would just have to skulk back to the dealer again.

I Wish You Were Running
From The Law

I love traveling. Alone. Escaping to the locales I've read about and imagined is a type of ecstasy for which I am usually packed a full month in advance. The notion of meeting people who look and speak differently, eating their food and negotiating their cobblestone streets or unpaved roads, is irresistible to me. The anonymity of being thousands of miles from home with nothing required of me is life at its best.

Whenever I leave for one of my long-planned, long-saved-up-for exotic vacations, invariably a girlfriend or sister will utter those dreaded words: *Maybe you'll meet somebody.* It is like the kiss of death. I don't WANT to meet somebody! I want to be left alone to wander foreign streets, ride foreign metros, eat foreign foods and get lost in great museums. That's all. Meeting somebody might mean having to spend time with that person, and be social, and sacrifice my treasured aloneness. But, on one particular Eastern European tour, after receiving the Kiss from a girlfriend, the worst that could happen did happen. But with a twist.

I'm not a fan of cruising for the obvious reason—the crowds that are herded like so many head of cattle from dining room to dance floor to Lido Bar and back again. But, for one with limited means and a long list of cities to visit, a cruise ship is a great mode of transportation. So, after searching long and hard for a reasonable package deal to St. Petersburg, Russia to get my Hermitage fix, I settled for a weeklong Scandinavian cruise that would put me in the grand city for two days. Leaving from Stockholm and stopping in Helsinki and Oslo, the itinerary would suit my needs perfectly.

Solo cruising is a fascinating phenomenon. First, you are punished and forced to pay a premium for being alone. (That is, unless you're on a singles cruise, which is a glorified meat market to be avoided like the plague.) Then, you're looked upon with pity and disdain by the staff, and targeted by ship retailers hawking already-overpriced knockoffs of designer hats and tee shirts and swimsuits and jewels. But, these indignities can be overcome if you know who and what to avoid, and plan accordingly.

Settling in for the main dining room's late seating, I was ready on that first night to meet those who would be my dining companions for the rest of the week. There was a family of four with two parents and two young adult children; a couple in their early 50s or so; and one other solo traveler, a man about five years older than I, decent looking with an easy smile. We all introduced ourselves, determined who was from where, and engaged in requisite small talk. Not too uncomfortable, and besides, the food was good and we were all seasoned wine drinkers. But then came the second night.

The family of four and the couple in their 50s were never to be seen again. The Man and I sat awkwardly side by side for awhile, waiting and hoping they would show. Then we relaxed, figuring we'd make the best of it. What shore excursions did you book? Have you cruised before? What ports have you visited? The conversation was good, so we went for a drink after dinner. The next night, we attended the Broadway Review together. The day after that, he switched his planned shore excursion and joined me for my first day in The Hermitage and Catherine's Palace. Oohing and aahing our way through the paintings of the masters, the long-anticipated Amber Room, and the silly, over-the-top gilded glory of it all, we became buds.

The ship's staff started treating us as a couple, replacing their pity with an enthusiastic stamp of approval. And so it went. We had a jolly old time, laughed comfortably, and talked seriously about philosophy, theology, history, and the Yankees. Nothing too personal, and nothing romantic. This was someone I enjoyed. I was comfortable, not at all put-upon, and my guarded personal space felt safe. I could easily accept The Man and me enjoying one another's friendship, if not companionship.

The week-long cruise was one of the best I'd taken, and I knew it was only partially because of the amazing locales. The Man and I had made each other's vacation more than what either of us had expected. There was nothing romantic, but there was a comfortable companionship that truly enhanced our holiday. And, the whole thing was good for my ego because I was reminded that, being a charming and witty conversationalist when I wanted to be, I could pretty much socialize with the best of them if called upon to do so. Such reminders are always a good barometer to ensure I haven't gone to the dark side of aloneness.

A funny thing happened on our final evening together. Well, two funny things. We sat in the atrium sipping Porto and watching people milling about in the open central area on decks above and below. It was an electric atmosphere, well-planned by the cruise line but a first-time thrill for so many travelers. There were seniors who were on their first and last vacation and wanted to milk the once-in-a-lifetime dream for all they could. Couples who'd drunk too much and gambled too much all week, but were still up for a raucous farewell bash. Exhausted parents of families who just wanted to get home and put their kids up for adoption. The Man and I watched, whispering and giggling like schoolgirls at the demeanor, mode of dress and alcohol consumption of everyone in sight. Then a flash mob broke out.

The cultural phenomenon had come and gone pretty quickly, with many of the public displays becoming so contrived that only the people in the mob even showed up. But this one was different. It was exactly what a flash mob should be, perfectly timed, well rehearsed, and completely unexpected. And The Man and I were right in the middle of it. Literally. From the first strains of Michael Jackson's Thriller, we watched as our bartender, a group of cabin stewards passing by, a maintenance man changing a light bulb, and about 20 people we thought were passengers, all fell into sync on two decks, up and down the giant spiral staircase, above, below, before and behind us. That was the first funny thing.

As the song ended and the mob dispersed, The Man turned to me with a serious look. We'd already exchanged email addresses and phone numbers and agreed to keep in touch (and I wasn't even lying about that).

I think it's time for me to tell you who I really am. Okay, what was going on? He hadn't said so directly, but my sense was that he was retired from an uneventful career that he just didn't care to talk about. Hobbies and travels had dominated our conversation about ourselves, and we knew only that we were both single and at least financially able to travel. I was content that he wasn't a fugitive from justice or some such thing. Now I looked at him blankly. Not sure what to expect, my eyes narrowed and I prepared for the worst.

I am a Catholic priest.

Whether it was the Porto, the thrill of Thriller, or the sheer absurdity of the situation, I cannot say. But, somewhere deep inside me, gently at first and then with a quaking that wouldn't stop, peals of rolling-on-the-floor laughter erupted. This was insane on so many levels. It couldn't have been any funnier if he had indeed been running from the law, but it might have been less shocking. But, what had I really expected? Anything? (Not this!)

He had no way of knowing it, but I was laughing at myself as much as at the situation. Whose life was this, anyway? Did this sort of thing happen to other people? Just when I was patting myself on the back for being able to be social and "normal," I find out that I'm dating a Catholic priest. (Well, sort of.) Who does that? The whole scene was just goofy enough to find its way into in my cosmic, comical, complicated Life Alone.

The Man joined my little party and together we laughed until tears rolled, all of the unasked questions and their ridiculous answers becoming funnier by the minute. There was no need to explain why he typically didn't offer up that bit of information when meeting folks in a social setting or when he just wanted to be anonymous. It was understandable. But ridiculous nonetheless.

He was going on to Prague and I spending an extra day in Stockholm. We did stay in touch, and still do today, and sometimes find ourselves laughing all over again when we remember that night. Even as a priest, he is a loner, and still enjoys anonymity when he travels just as

I do. But, our experience has caused him to rethink being too secretive about his identity.

As I headed back to my cabin to pack, I considered for maybe the zillionth time on what planet I must be living. Oh, that's right, it was Planet Carla. Where middle-aged women pick up Catholic priests and find themselves in the middle of flash mobs on cruise ships. Couldn't wait to call my girlfriend with the news that I had, indeed, met someone.

You Called Me Here Today
To Tell Me What?

There came an especially good time in my Life Alone, when I was content and at peace, thriving in my career and enjoying friendships that respected my frequent need for solitude. I call these the-days-of-driving-in-my-car-singing-loudly.

Music is one of my greatest joys. Old rock makes me happy. Jazz and blues get me into a groove. Country at once makes me sad and cracks me up. Classical brings peace, and sometimes tears at its sheer beauty. But Motown—aah, Motown. The first notes of *My Girl* or *Where Did Our Love Go?* are all it takes to trigger those automatic, electric reactions of cranking up the volume, clearing my throat, and transporting myself back in time.

Unlike my mom, who sang hymns around the house all the time, I only sing in the privacy of my car. But I sing loudly, passionately, facial expressions and all. If I am stopped at a red light, I might even close my eyes and throw my head back. I know people are watching, but I don't care. It is one of those activities that signal I am at a good place in life, and I embrace it with everything I have.

During those particular days-of-driving-in-my-car-singing-loudly, I was dating a little, usually just casual, one-time coffee or lunch dates. But one day I met a gentleman whose choice for a first date made quite an impression on me (not an easy feat), leaving me curious and wanting to see him again.

One of the things I've always loved about New Mexico is its big sky, yielding the most amazing sunrises and sunsets I've seen anywhere in the world. When viewing them from the balcony of my foothills home, there was an aura of heavenly peace and unmatched beauty. I embraced any opportunity to escape life's rigors and submerge in this other-worldly splendor. This first date from above would be such an opportunity.

He was a local ophthalmologist with whom I'd enjoyed several weeks of conversation, laughter and discovery after our online introduction. We'd read the same obscure books and shared many of the same loner-centric ideas of life. He, too, seemed to be living A Life Alone. When the time came to meet in person, I knew he would come up with something good. He'd lived in the region over 20 years, I only five, so there was much I was still anxious to discover.

New Mexico's vineyards and wineries were an enigma, really. At least, to me they were. I had never visited a vineyard, but I'd enjoyed New Mexico wines since moving to the state, and I was amazed at the quality. The Doc had mentioned he held a membership to one of the oldest wineries in the area, and our first date was to include dinner, wine-tasting and a tour of the facility. When he gave me directions, I immediately knew it was in a pure-old-west, quaint and unspoiled part of Albuquerque, the part that existed at the center of my love for the region.

The winery was tucked behind the vineyard, unseen from the road. Driving through the tall foliage that late afternoon, the sense of peace immediately enveloped me. I stopped at a small parking lot and walked a deserted path through another section of vineyard, as if finding my way through a tall maze. Arriving at the surprising, sprawling grounds, I found The Doc standing in the doorway of a pueblo-style structure. We recognized each other immediately and shared a quick, comfortable hug.

What I had thought was a quaint side building turned out to be a massive, open expanse of leather sofas, lounge chairs and small bistro tables positioned far enough away from each other for patrons to have privacy. The late afternoon sun shone on Saltillo tiles through several large skylights. In a far corner was a small bar where a young man in an apron was talking quietly with a group of five or six people. We made our way over to try a couple of the Cabs he was pouring. It was the kind of wine tasting you might enjoy in your living room.

Continuing on through what turned out to be a lavish private home that was open for tours (only to those with premium memberships, it turned out), we arrived at one of several small, private patios and settled into lounge chairs. The Doc pointed past the vineyard I'd walked through, to another larger patio where several diners were laughing and talking. *That's where you have to stay if you don't spring for the premium package.* I envisioned those poor people, looking longingly at our patio, wondering what perks we were enjoying. They were the riff-raff, relegated by limited means to the outskirts of nirvana.

We ordered dinner and a bottle of Pinot as the sun began to set. The sky was pink, the air clean and soft. The Doc detailed the rich history of the vineyard, the winery, and the family that had built it nearly 100 years earlier. As the evening unfolded, I knew already that I wanted a second date. And I would get one.

He called two days after the winery. I'd received an email the day before, the usual easy banter, saying how much he'd enjoyed the date. Now he wanted to get together for an evening at the Kimo Theater, a favorite haunt for both us that offered up quirky indie, noir, and classic films often attended by only a handful of folks. We'd both been surprised that we'd never run into each other there before. We would meet that weekend to catch part of the Hitchcock in HD festival.

I'd only met The Doc once, but our conversations were pleasant, we laughed easily together, and I felt he could be a friend who could add flavor to my life. And perform eye surgery should the need arise.

After the movie, we strolled the downtown Albuquerque streets for awhile before deciding where to stop for a bite. It was the city's verve center, older and less contrived than Nob Hill, with parked squad cars there to remind one of the lurking dangers that just added to the energy. We ducked into a tiny Italian place, ordered wine and began poring over a sparse but impressive menu. The Doc placed his on the table and looked directly at me. He apparently had something to say.

This is amazing. I can't believe how content I am with you. Hmm. "Content with you." Interesting choice of words. Since meeting him I'd believed that, like me, he'd met people online and rejected them all, arriving at an early conclusion that contentment was to be found alone and not in the company of others.

I'm really interested in you, Carla, he went on. *I know it's early to talk about a romantic relationship, but I want you to think about something. I want to go forward with this. But I do still see my ex-wife, and the other lady I met online. How would you feel about that?*

I'd been watching him intently, wondering where he was going with this. I kept watching him intently. Just what kind of crack was this guy smoking?

If you're a single guy or gal in the dating scene, here's a word to the wise: When you want to break up with someone, or take a breather from someone, or tell someone you want them to be one of a collection of paramours, don't invite them on a date to do it. Call them. E-mail them. Text them. I know this is contrary to traditional etiquette, but trust me. They won't want you to see their face during such an exchange.

I turned down The Doc's generous offer to add me to his menagerie. I still wasn't sure if I wanted a romantic relationship at all, but if I did, I knew it would have to be exclusive. I guess I'd taken for granted that all loners felt this way about such relationships, but I was wrong. Like any other group, loners cannot be pigeonholed and must not be stereotyped. I chalked it up to another learning experience and, cancelling my application for premium winery membership, I quietly resumed my journey through the-days-of-driving-in-my-car-singing-loudly.

Anti-Social Networking

Whenever there is something or someone new in my life, I get the same goofy question from several people: *Where'd you meet? Where'd you find that? Online?* Okay, granted, that's how it's done these days. But why? When did it become a given that if you met *any* new person, or found a great new job or apartment, it had to have been online?

Early in my career, I noticed people in the industry bandying about a new catchword. *Networking.* In those days, it usually involved showing up at happy hour somewhere, getting plastered and exchanging a few business cards. But then it became a science. Folks got strategic in planning which events to attend, determining where the right people would be, and wooing other movers and shakers to such events. They actually conducted business meetings, and didn't get drunk. Work got done, people found the jobs they wanted and made the connections they needed. It was a beautiful thing. And that's when I joined the fray. Business opportunities without having to be particularly social? I was all in.

But, it didn't take long before the whole thing came full circle, and people were mixing dating with networking, and gossiping with networking, and partying with networking. The lines became blurred, and I retreated once again. And then came the Web.

I embraced emailing, and certainly loved uploading documents and manuscripts rather than snail-mailing them. But soon, that little piece of heaven was spoiled, too, when people with nothing else to do began forwarding every shred of nonsense they received online. (And, of course, when I asked to be removed from mailing lists, I was branded unfriendly and anti-social. After all, what was wrong with me? How could

I not find those piano-playing kittens funny?)

Still sulking over the bastardization of my inbox, when MySpace came along I completely ignored it. I never really knew what it was supposed to accomplish, but there didn't seem to be any point to it that could benefit me. Then came Facebook. The dreaded Facebook. Overnight, it seemed, otherwise rational people were spending hours on end reading inane summaries of walks in the park, head colds, hangnails, and babies' first steps. It was as if some parallel universe had cropped up and everyone was flocking to it.

Do you remember the classic Twilight Zone episode called *To Serve Man*? Space aliens had landed on earth. They were deemed friendly and readily accepted by earth governments, partially because they came bearing a book with that title name. As giddy earthlings boarded the spaceship for a "tour" of the aliens' home planet, scientists had finally been able to translate the book and made a horrifying discovery. The episode ends with one of the scientists calling desperately to her colleague as he boards the spaceship: *Don't get on the ship! It's a cookbook!*

That was my view of Facebook. I was certain that young Mark Zuckerberg had written a cookbook full of addictive recipes that would make us all appear better and brighter and healthier and yummier—only to be devoured in the end. Besides, if I wanted to be friends with people I went to high school with, I would be. But, if I haven't seen you in 30 years, and I've been okay with that, chances are I don't miss you and I don't want you to "find" me.

I dug in my heels and refused the phenomenon. I didn't understand it all, and I didn't want to. But, with the publication of my third book in 2009, a friend convinced me that Facebook would be a wonderful marketing tool. I became suspicious as she made the case. She was cleverly omitting the caveat that, once you're out there, you're out there forever. In a momentary lapse, I bit the bullet and set up a page. I was dumbstruck at the instant bombardment. With shock and awe, everyone I'd ever met joined forces in full armor to crash their Sherman-tank-like world violently into mine. *Never mind, never mind!!* was my silent, panic-stricken shriek. *I don't want this!*

The assortment of characters terrified me. Schoolmates, co-workers, old acquaintances, ex-spouses, stalkers, scammers, you name it, many whom I'd never met but for some reason wanted to be my friend, all competing for my attention. Their voices were so loud, and they were all talking at the same time, and arguing, and joking, and crying. I'd been told the best thing about Facebook was using it in the privacy and quiet of your own home. But this didn't feel private or quiet at all. They were all right there in my living room, yelling at me with their indiscriminate use of caps and punctuation. I cried. What had I done?

Taking the page down was a monumental undertaking, and even when I thought it was done, my brother assured me months later that I did indeed still have a page, because he had just sent me a message. I never went on Facebook again, so to this day I don't know if I have a page. I don't care.

What baffles me is the absolute inability of the majority of the world to communicate in any other way. When colleagues learn that I'm not on Facebook, there's always a suspicious, sidelong glance, as if to suggest I must surely be hiding something because why else would I not want to open up my entire life to the entire world?

There's a similar incapacity in our society to meet a romantic interest by any other means. Initially, this is a little less baffling, because people can impress the heck out of a prospective partner online. But, then comes judgment day when you have to come clean and admit that you're not a supermodel or a brainiac, and the photo in your profile was taken in college. So, the question remains, Why?

It seemed counter-intuitive, but I liked the anonymity of online dating. It suited my distaste for in-person initial meetings from which I usually needed to extricate myself pretty quickly anyway. And I considered myself a pretty perceptive person who could spot a fraud a mile away, so I had the luxury of deciding, right or wrong, that so many people would not be a good fit for me, without having to meet them. (Granted, I wasn't accustomed to such practiced, accomplished frauds, who had apparently hired equally accomplished writers to prepare convincing profiles that would fool even the most skeptical among us.)

I met a wide array of characters. There was The Doc. There was the Stanford grad who was also a libertarian outlaw. (I eventually concluded that he'd probably graduated from Stanford Community College.) There was a university professor, and an engineer who also turned out to be a cyber-stalker. But, even after a couple of years (on and off), I would still renew my membership every now and then just to see who was new. Besides, I knew that even if I met someone on one of my rare excursions out of the house, it wasn't very likely that I would actually talk to him. Online, I could be as ornery as I pleased, blocking and deleting would-be suitors at will, hiding my profile, or just ignoring their messages altogether. In fact, after a while I had myself thoroughly convinced that online dating was the God-given miracle anticipated by mankind for eons.

It's not going away. In fact, it's bound to get worse. And, even today, I still re-up periodically. So, is the whole online-dating-social-networking phenomenon a wonderful invention or a horrible blight on our society and our children's future? Yes. Most definitely.

Heroes

Call me jaded, but there are few people who captivate me. I've never been impressed by how much money you make or how many letters are behind your name. What fascinates me most are the decisions people make for themselves in life, and how they own and walk out those decisions, right or wrong. People who are not bound by tradition or the expectations of others. These are loners by virtue of their refusal to be beholden to any crowd or institution. Their independent spirit is often honed over a lifetime of tough decisions and consequences.

I once met a trio of friends whose unusual choices had yielded both good and bad results, but whose subsequent lifestyles were most intriguing.

Giovanna is a nuclear physicist, educated in her native Italy. As a young scientist, she met and fell in love with a colleague. He was already married, and she already engaged to another, but their love story was the stuff of which epic tales are written. He divorced his wife and moved from Paris to Rome to be with his beloved. She ended her engagement and embraced a love forbidden by her family. But that wasn't new for Giovanna. She'd already nixed the family tradition of foregoing higher education and devoting herself to marrying early and having lots of kids. She remembers her appalled parents who already saw no reason for her academic pursuits, but nearly passed out when she told them her field of study. *But, it's too difficult! Why would you want to do this? You can never be successful at it!* (Gee, thanks.) But science was her passion, and if she was going to do it at all, she was going to be all in, both academically and professionally.

Giovanna defied tradition and made a life with her new love. They never married, but they grew together. Then apart. After the birth of their only child, their careers burgeoned and life became settled, perhaps too settled for the system-bucking Giovanna. Ever-curious, she made reading an art form. And dedicated, there was so much more she wanted to accomplish professionally. But her love was drifting in the opposite direction, wanting to take his little family and escape the rigors of their world of science and success. And so they did. The two avid sailors owned a boat, and it would play a crucial role in the radical decisions that would shape their future.

During their daughter's tenth year, the little clan made the big decision to check out of society for a year. They would live aboard the boat, sailing from Virginia to South America, forgetting about science and work and bureaucracy, enjoying one another and seeing what else life held for them. Deep down, Giovanna knew their ultimate goals differed. For her, it was a sabbatical. For him, a new life. He would never again return to the life of world-renowned scientist.

At first, the adventure was in keeping with so many others she'd made in her march to her own drumbeat. But, during that year, she knew. The love story was over. She would eventually make her way back to her country home in Italy, and soon thereafter return for a second stint with a major lab in the U.S. As her ex-partner stubbornly dug in his heels, willing only to embrace the hermit's life aboard the boat, Giovanna's responsibilities grew. The next years would mean custody battles, compromises that involved footing the bill for many of his travel expenses, and convincing her family and herself that her decisions were the right ones. For Giovanna, it was all pretty cut and dried. Her child, her career, and her independence were her priorities, and all that remained was to do what was necessary to preserve them.

The Life Alone always comes with a price. The choices we make, our priorities in life, must be so important to us that we're willing to sacrifice that which may be only a little less important. Such was the case in Bledi's life.

Growing up in Albania in the 90s was grim at best. And, as the middle child of a single mom in his poverty-stricken homeland, Bledi's existence was more difficult than most. A bully for an older brother and an innocent for a younger sister drove him deep into an introspective, creative childhood, with an uncanny understanding of cutting-edge computer technology and the foresight to know it would be his lifeline. As a teen, he would sit amazed and amused, listening to his mom and aunts in the next room expressing their confidence that the jailbird older brother would be a success, but concern that the soft-spoken, slightly-built Bledi could ever make it in life. This, despite the entrepreneurial spirit that allowed the young man to talk his way into tech positions and even start his own business—and support his family.

Upon his release from prison, older brother resumed his bullying ways. And Bledi began putting in place a plan of escape. His family laughed at the idea, but didn't dampen his resolve. In the third grade he'd been given a choice to study Russian or English. He chose English, and became fluent over several years. When the Peace Corps set up shop in Albania, the enterprising 19-year-old walked into their headquarters and offered his services as a translator and tutor. After joining the humanitarian group, the relationships he cultivated would lead to a student visa and enrollment at Minnesota State University

Moorhead, carrying a double major of computer science and graphic communications.

All was well in Bledi's unassuming life in America, until the next two monumental decisions he would have to make. The first was thrust upon him, but would cause him to go looking for the second. A call from a distant female relative already living in the U.S., and a request that Bledi donate a kidney to her husband, made for an unimaginable life choice. But, when push came to shove, the choice wasn't so difficult for Bledi. *I had an opportunity to save a life. The guy had been on the transplant list for years, and I was his last hope.* (I often wonder what I would have done, given the same choice. I have a feeling I would still be in possession of both of my kidneys.)

The time it took to prep for and undergo the surgery would end the young man's visa term and deplete his savings. And so arrived the next big decision. He needed to find a way to stay in the U.S. and complete his education. Ignoring the rest of the world and retreating into his private thoughts and research, the only thing he could come up with was to join the military. A diminutive Albanian with one kidney and an expiring visa? Not a problem. His feverish determination landed him in the little-known Military Accessions Vital to the National Interest (MAVNI) program, where he would serve for years as a helicopter pilot and mechanic.

To Bledi, it wasn't about some great accomplishment or having a pat-myself-on-the-back-because-I-proved-my-family-wrong moment. It was simply the logical choice. I asked him if he ever felt lonely during those years of tough choices. The question had never occurred to him. For this hero of A Life Alone, it was all about pragmatism. Like Giovanna, he knew what he wanted to accomplish and quietly went about figuring out how to do it, notwithstanding establishment, protocol, or the opinions of others. So did Navi.

Until I met her, I'd only encountered one other person who'd been in an arranged marriage. Navi's was probably the worst argument ever for the institution. She arrived in the U.S. from her native India after only having spoken a few times to her betrothed. She discovered his ongoing infidelity almost immediately, as married life in a strange country and in the household of in-laws unfolded.

Two children later, Navi was keenly aware of one thing. Her education and IT expertise were the gold mine that would set her free. Now came decision time.

The job offer came from Virginia. She was well settled into life in Atlanta at the time, great career, kids doing well in school. And a loveless marriage to a philandering husband. The divorce was a shock that Navi's parents wouldn't overcome for years, and they spent those years letting her know as much every chance they got. But, the decision to give her husband custody of the children while she was under a two-year contract in Virginia? What decent, self-respecting Indian woman did that?

He is a great parent and the kids have a wonderful home, she told me. They spend summers and holidays with her and, though she misses them desperately, she knows her decision was right for them and for her. Radical and rebellious, yes, but it was a loner's decision, one that Navi alone fully understood. And that was enough for her.

Someone I respected a great deal once warned me that when we are called to our place in life, when we receive that calling that will help determine what is in us and whom we will be, we will receive it alone. No one else will get it, and no one else will *get* it. But no one has to. Many will argue against it, call us crazy, question our foolish folly. But, we must walk our walk alone. We must make the tough decisions and live with them. There may be few who have the fortitude to walk the walk of this calling, but those who do are my heroes.

I Was Born This Way

I'm always fascinated when observing my two granddaughters, whether interacting with each other, with friends, or playing alone. They fascinate me not only because they're my granddaughters, but because they are polar opposites.

Zoe, the oldest, is much like her Mimi was as a girl. Her own person, a little fastidious is some areas, brooding at times, and likes things "just so." Troy, on the other hand, just doesn't give a damn. She's a mover and a shaker, gregarious and joyous and unapologetic. Both are loners, because each one marches to her own tune.

So, is it nature or nurture? What makes one a loner? To what do we owe that deep-seated need to spend great chunks of time with self, musing and pondering the things of life (or just of the day)? Why do two little girls, borne of the same parents, grow up in the same household but to different drumbeats? There's been no shortage of research, but the best minds in the business still haven't reached a common conclusion. So, I turned to even better minds, those of everyday folks, to make some sense of it all. Freelance writer and parent Kori Rodley Irons wrote this post on the subject for Families.com:

I have written before about "joiners and loners" and how challenging it can be for parents and children when their social temperaments do not match. But, it occurred to me that we parents have a tendency to think that we can change and mold our children more than we probably can. Some children are just natural extroverts or introverts and it is as much about temperament and personality as anything else. In this day and age when being labeled a "loner" can be cause for concern about one's antisocial tendencies, it might behoove us to remember that some children are just naturally and healthily loners.

It is completely normal for a child to want to spend time alone and, for very imaginative children, they actually might prefer big doses of alone time where they can play, imagine, create worlds and stories, read, etc.

Of course, parents can strive to introduce balance and make sure that children get the opportunity to develop social skills and make friends—but a child who is more of a loner may prefer one or two good, like-minded friends to the bustle of parties and groups. This is okay. As long as we stay involved and watch out for signs of distress or red flags that might indicate something larger than temperament is at play, we may just need to adjust and embrace the individual social style of our child.

I think Irons is on to something. Her common sense assessment of children's tendencies toward aloneness is probably accurate. It's also worth noting that most young children do not have the capacity to consciously determine to conduct themselves in one manner or another, at least not for more than a few minutes. (And, of course, there are traits found in those living A Life Alone that are considered pretty weird—you just can't make this stuff up and decide you're going to be that way!)

In my own case, I didn't just wake up one day and decide I was going to go my own way. The tendencies to do so were already in me. The only decisions to be made were how those tendencies would manifest, and, in many cases, even that was not up to me.

There are certainly times when nurture comes into play. Some children who grow up without siblings, are homeschooled, or may not be exposed to much social activity for various reasons, will become comfortable entertaining themselves (and often become the most creative among us). They may remain loners for life. Or, they may not. My own son, who was an only child, is an independent thinker to be sure, but still popular and comfortable in social environments. Similarly, children who are raised in large families with lots of social interaction may be given to the lifestyle of social butterfly in adulthood. Or not.

So, is it nurture or nature? I lean more toward nature. But, either way, we may want to consider giving our kids a little more slack. Yes, they're expected to adhere to certain social norms, but within that big picture, let's try just letting them be who they are—whoever that might be. No doubt we'll be pleasantly surprised at the very cool contributions they'll be able to make, and the creative people they will become, when set free to be themselves.

Traveling Mercies

I am still bedazzled by the newness of spring. Not typically a great optimist, I become one when warm weather rolls around. Winter's disappointments are forgotten, creativity is awakened and hope in all things is restored. And each year, I look forward to indulging certain ritual behaviors.

First, I change something. Determined to bring something new into my life to match the new season, I will adopt a color, maybe yellow, and incorporate a touch of it into my wardrobe each day; sometimes my new behavior involves a short, short haircut, or wearing flats for the entire season.

(This year it's headbands. Admittedly, there are days when it's hard to tell if I'm headed to work or the tennis court, but I don't care. I'm rocking my headbands until summer comes.)

The second ritual behavior is planning a vacation. A long, exotic trek to the other side of the world. It may not be taken for a while; it may require more than a year's savings. But, the planning of it is where the journey begins.

A tour through Italy was the culmination of one of these spring flings. Memorable for more reasons than I can name here, those two weeks were also the time when I met a particular reluctant loner with whom I've remained close ever since. I was boarding a tour bus in Florence. Visitors from around the world crammed in and, when I managed to find the last empty seat, I turned to greet the woman next to me. Maybe in her early 60s, she was soft-spoken and clearly not too comfortable. I was curious and struck up a conversation, something I never do and wasn't sure why I was doing that day.

Uma and her husband had planned their Mediterranean vacation for years. Both Canadian criminal court judges, their demanding work schedules and family obligations had allowed them little time for such an escape, but as retirement approached, so did their opportunity. They dreamed of seeing the Vatican, cruising the Greek Isles, and so much more. And then he died, two months after retiring. Crushed and alone, and never having traveled, Uma had some tough decisions to make. The fearless loner deep within prevailed, and she soon found herself boarding a flight for Rome. So, there she sat on a crowded tour bus, terrified but there. I was so proud of her!

We became close on that tour, and now it's hard to keep Uma home. At least a couple of times a year I'll get an email from my Canadian compadre, asking if I'm free to join her on a tour of this country or that. This is the good stuff about travel. These are the positives of A Life Alone, ever-elusive but often found in interaction with others from another place, others who are not like you but, in so many ways, are exactly like you.

While these intercontinental jaunts are the center of my personal life, domestic travels are a regular occurrence in my professional world. In some ways, they're more eventful than the foreign trips. First, there is the work that demands my concentration, so I don't have the luxury of just experiencing the journey and letting life happen. And, there are always issues from the start— an inability to sit in a middle seat on a plane (not a mere dislike for the middle seat, but an actual physical illness at the thought of having people in such close proximity on either side of me); then there's the need to sanitize the tray table and armrest, as fellow passengers watch and begin to wonder God-knows-what; and, of course, there's that whole bringing –a–change–of–sheets–and–remaking–my– hotel–room–bed–before–I–can–sleep–in–it thing—after sanitizing everything in the room that any other person may have touched or even looked at. Granted, these things take time and energy, but they are *my things,* so they're okay. What's not okay is *other people's things.* And, if you travel much, you know that other people's things are visited upon you wherever you go.

Strange things happen on Planet Carla, so whenever I'm traveling, it's safe to assume that hijinks will ensue. There even came a time when my co-workers began anticipating my return from business trips because they knew I'd come bearing a most unbelievable story. Like the girl on the flight to Chicago...

She was one of a large group, a sports team of some sort, all teens with pimples and braces and cell phones, oblivious to the world around them. They lounged in the Albuquerque Sunport eating junk food and texting friends who were sitting right next to them. I eyed them warily, thinking how much I preferred even babies over teens on a flight.

The Girl had been mindlessly munching on Doritos from a large bag sitting in her lap. Then she reached into her backpack and pulled out a yellow bag of M&Ms, the peanut kind. She never stopped texting with her left thumb.

When the flight delay was announced, the group didn't seem to mind at all. I'm not even sure they ever heard it. They just kept eating. The Girl had finished the M&Ms and returned to the Doritos. I was mesmerized.

Ninety minutes later, we boarded. I found a window seat in the sixth row, cleaned my surroundings and pulled out my iPad. An older man took the aisle seat, and a younger one settled in the middle. As Group C finally straggled aboard, the first few teens made their way to the back of the aircraft. Still unfazed, still texting, still eating. I glanced up to see The Girl at the front of the cabin. She wasn't texting, or smiling any longer. Her skin tone appeared to have a greenish tint. *Please, God, no,* I implored. This wasn't really going to happen, was it? It was.

She began making her way down the aisle, but stopped at Row 6. Doubling over and holding her belly, she lost the M&Ms, the Doritos, and apparently everything else she'd eaten in the past week. Vomit splashed the older gentlemen in the aisle seat, and everyone in the surrounding aisle seats. The younger guy in the middle was practically in my lap. The line behind The Girl dispersed, but she chose to continue to the back of the plane once she was done, probably out of sheer mortification.

The sickening odor wafted through the plane, but lingered most pungently in Row 6. Within minutes, Southwest Airlines personnel had boarded, with...could it be? Not a wet vac, but...paper towels?! The passengers sat stunned. The Girl had disappeared to the rear of the plane. I sank deeper into my seat, closed my eyes and made a mental comparison of this fiasco with my last trip...

The flight arrived late into Norfolk, and I had to make my way over to Hampton. Tomorrow would be my first day of orientation at my new place of work in Virginia. I was to be in town for two weeks, then fly back to Albuquerque for a short respite before next month's trip to Vietnam. A lot going on but, still not feeling especially stressed, I was anxious to see what Virginia had in store.

By the time I checked into my hotel it was 10 p.m. I needed to iron a blouse, but it would wait until morning. Exhausted, I went right to bed, planning on getting my ideal seven hours of zzzzzs. It was not to be.

The smoke alarm pierced my slumber at approximately 3:30 a.m. But it sounded different. After determining that my room was not on fire, I peered through the peephole to see people milling about. Some were headed for the stairs. Then I realized it wasn't just my smoke alarm, but every alarm on the entire floor, maybe the entire hotel. Hesitant to flee into the night in my PJs, I tried to assess the situation. I cracked open the door and saw others doing the same, trying to determine if there was really a fire. I went back in and looked through the window at the parking lot three floors below, where maybe 50 people were shivering in their nightclothes. I was having none of it. But the smoke alarm seemed to be getting louder, shrieking, piercing, drilling into my skull. I decided to iron a blouse.

I'd seen it happen before. It was probably just a system malfunction, the piercing would stop any minute now, and the cold people in the parking lot would return to their rooms. I would just take a quick shower, get dressed, and find an early morning diner for breakfast before my office opened. While the iron heated, I stood on the bed and tried to at least dismantle my smoke alarm, but to no avail. There was commotion outside my door, then a heavy knock. I had a sinking feeling I was in big trouble. *Yes?* I inquired sweetly, innocently. Then I saw them through the peephole.

Standing impatiently at the door, calling out to anyone who might be inside, were three burly firefighters in full regalia—with axes. Was this really happening? The instant I cracked the door, they rushed in, the angry hotel manager in hot pursuit. And they attacked me. All four of them.

Ma'am, you're not supposed to be here. Do you understand that you are supposed to evacuate when you hear a smoke alarm? Do you have any idea what it's like to pull a body from a burning building?

I got the worst of it from the manager. *Are you crazy? This hotel could be burning down, and you're up in here ironing. Did you vandalize that smoke alarm?*

The lashing was well-deserved, so I took it without fighting back. These people had a job to do, and I was upsetting their apple cart. I silently obeyed their orders. Fortunately, the malfunction was corrected before I had to join the shivering losers in the parking lot. This would be one for the books, for sure. But then there was that deserted hotel in Fargo that had me thinking I was in The Shining; the hydroplaning incident in Philly; and, of course, the tornado in Jacksonville...

I arrived in Florida to welcoming, sunny skies. It would be a quick trip, just one meeting in Jacksonville and then a drive up to Brunswick, Georgia the next day for a second meeting. As I settled into my room to look over some files, I checked the weather. Rain was predicted overnight, but no matter.

I awoke to overcast skies and pouring rain, but still wasn't too concerned. Until I turned on the television and heard an anxious weather woman offering up dire warnings of tornadoes touching down throughout the region. *What??!* I had a pretty long drive ahead of me and decided it might just be time to get concerned.

The weather map was an array of colors indicating where the worst storms were, and where tornadoes were likely to touch down. A dark purplish path ran from Jacksonville, Florida to Brunswick, Georgia. *Oh, great. Do I stay or do I go?* I had worked for months to get the Brunswick appointment. I prayed, but wasn't sure I was hearing any answers. At that moment I decided to venture out and, if things looked ugly, I could always turn back.

The driving rains were blinding, and the wind blew the rental car slightly. I was still 50 miles out, but the car radio wasn't reporting anything too terrible up ahead. I came upon the Brunswick exit sooner than I expected, and breathed a sigh of relief. Winding my way through surface streets at my GPS's direction, I came within a half-mile of the office building I sought when I felt a jolt and heard a loud *pop*. It was just a pothole, but something had struck my tire and instantly flattened it. I pulled over to a nearby parking lot just as someone on the radio breathlessly announced that tornadoes were touching down in Brunswick. I grabbed my phone to call AAA. It was frozen. Not dead, frozen. I took the battery out and pushed it back, trying everything I knew to restart it. Then it rang, and the caller's name appearing on the screen was the executive I was scheduled to meet with in 20 minutes. But nothing happened when I tried to answer it. I looked around at the deserted streets, sheets of rain impairing my vision. This was not going to be good.

After several more attempts to get my phone to work, I gave up, grabbed my briefcase and good-for-nothing umbrella, and started making my way to the office building. As the elevator door opened into the suite that was my destination, a woman rushed to me. *You must be Carla. We've been trying to call you to tell you we're closing the office because of the tornadoes. We...* She stopped short and stared in disbelief. And there I stood, a scary-looking, disheveled, wet woman from the west, hair matted, mascara running, soaked to the skin. I smiled at her, only later realizing how macabre that smile must have looked.

She and her assistant were the only ones left in the office, and they wanted to leave. I didn't let them. I'd come to do a presentation and I was going to do it. They rushed to get me paper towels and tea, and I took advantage of the opportunity, ignoring their anxiety. Thirty minutes later, I calmly asked to use their phone. And they would have to wait with me another 30 minutes until AAA arrived.

Such are the adventures of travel on Planet Carla. But, it's a good planet. It is many things, but never dull. Traveling alone, whether for business or pleasure, comes with great risk and great reward. It is not for the faint of heart. But, if you are living A Life Alone, it can be one of the most gratifying aspects of that life.

There is a common prayer in the Christian church for "traveling mercies" when someone is going on a trip, and I pray such mercies for myself each time I set out. Because I am here today, in one piece, thinking back over the mishaps and mayhem of my many journeys, it occurs to me that those prayers have never gone unanswered.

Fine Wine

I was an asthmatic child, suffering frequent severe attacks that landed me in the ER more times than I care to remember. But, by about the age of 12, I grew out of it. I would still have occasional shortness of breath, allergy issues and the like, but I would have only one more asthma attack in my life, twenty years later, the week my husband died. And never again.

As diseases go, asthma is pretty amazing. You just grow out of it. You get better as you get older. What else is like it? Acne?

Growth is an interesting word. It can be good or bad. It can be progress, or it can be a tumor. We typically grow out of things, but rarely grow into things. But, we have the power to change that. We get to choose what we will become, and whether we will grow better.

It is said that good wine can get better with age, and can continue to improve for years. But, there are conditions, including acidity and tannin levels, and fruit content. Sometimes, if the aging process is too prolonged, the wine can become more like vinegar. Also, not all wines will improve at all with age. The process is so fascinating that surely there must be life lessons we can glean from it. Or, at very least, we can have fun trying.

As with wine, before we can grow better we have to know what we have to work with. (Once again, the importance of knowing who we really are, and what we really want, comes into play.) Then we have to stay engaged, and be careful not to push any one lifestyle or habit too far. We must keep an eye on ourselves, never resting on our laurels, but making sure we are indeed actually growing *into* something. If we decide to live A Life Alone, but take that to mean just being alone and not actually living, creating, progressing, then we'll become as bitter as vinegar. It is an ever-present danger, especially for loners.

I became a tennis buff in my 20s. I just loved the game, and couldn't get enough of it. Soon after I got hooked on the game, I taught myself to play by watching the greats, and I actually became an okay player (albeit with the weirdest looking serve you've ever seen, but I could still hold my own). I always told myself I would take lessons one day, but it wasn't until my mid-50s that I actually did. What those lessons taught me was shocking.

Over time, I had taught my body what I thought it should do on the tennis court. I had trained my muscles to hit a ground stroke a certain way, and my feet and legs to move and chase down balls a certain way. Even my hands believed a particular racquet position was correct. And, they were all wrong. My body had grown strong and agile, but it had not grown *into* a correct understanding of the mechanics of the game of tennis. It knew what it was supposed to do, but not how to do it most efficiently and effectively. It would have to be retrained. It turned out

I would need a lot more lessons than I'd bargained for.

Such is life. Sometimes we get comfortable with things or habits just because it's the way we've always done them. Then, upon further examination, we may find that we're not comfortable at all. It may not even be what we really want to be doing, or we may not be getting the results we really want, but we keep at it just because. Here is where we would do well to remember Einstein's definition of insanity: doing the same thing over and over again, and expecting different results.

I would guess that the great majority of Americans are given to this type of behavior. We tend to make ironclad life choices and then refuse to reconsider them, even if they're not working for us. Or, we set goals, then work toward those goals until we've *arrived.* Neither of these behaviors constitutes growth in the positive sense. (What would happen if, whenever we feel as if we've accomplished something, we just stop? Stop working? Stop trying? Stop living?) Whether it's due to laziness, a lack of creativity to come up with a new path for ourselves, or just plain stubbornness, we are still robbing ourselves of the opportunity to grow.

As a die-hard lover of the Life Alone, I am committed to a certain lifestyle, but what that lifestyle looks like from year to year can vary widely. The life choice doesn't change, but how I walk it out does. When I decided to take ballroom dance lessons, they came with the expectation that I would show up once a week, partner with another dancer, and engage in inherently social behavior— listening to music, physical contact, talking and laughing (with others, no less!) Then, the group would go out for a drink or meet informally on another night for dinner. I could easily have said, *no, this doesn't fit with my lifestyle,* and nixed the whole idea. But, I would not have grown into the mediocre ballroom dancer that I am today.

One of the items near the top of my bucket list is to perform in community theater. Who knows why? It flies in the face of everything that I stand for. But, I've always wanted to do it. Not as a career or hobby, mind you, but just one production, one performance. And, one day I will. It may involve the same social interaction as my dance lessons, and it may be uncomfortable at first, but it will also involve growth, and therein lies the fulfillment—determining who and what I will grow *into.*

For me, continuing to grow all the days of my life is a critical pursuit. If I am allotted a certain amount of time on this earth, and I choose to use only a portion of it constructively, then I won't be "done" at the end of my time. I'll be half-baked, never fully realizing what I might have done or become, whose life I might have touched, what contribution I might have made. For most people, growth may not mean doing a clumsy tango on Friday nights or checking off a list of museums around the world to be visited. But, it's important to determine what it *does* look like in each of our lives.

Consider also our Maker. Might he be insulted if he gives us, say, 80 years, and we decide only to use 60 of them? Or, if we've been given a big, beautiful world, and we have no interest in 90 percent of it? As a parent and a grandparent, I would be insulted if I prepared a delicious four-course meal for my family but they were only interested in the rice. My greater concern would not be my hurt feelings, but that *they* were missing out on something so wonderful. Whatever our experiences in life, no matter the tough choices, bad decisions, the hurts and hang-ups, or the guaranteed unfairness of it all, there always remains something wonderful.

It's a great adventure, our time here. It's a cross between the daily unexpected events that are out of our control but leave us pleasantly surprised (or terribly shocked); and the conscious decisions we make for ourselves, not always knowing what their outcome will be. It's sort of like being on a lifelong African safari or world tour. We never quite know what's around the corner, and we may not like the next stop, but it's an adventure nonetheless. It will be many things, but it should never be dull.

And, here's the cool part. Even if we feel we have no control at all over the adventure, we can still enhance it at our choosing and shape it into what we want it to be. Whether living A Life Alone, one fraught with noise and companionship, or something in between, we must know that there is more we can add to it. There is always more of the good stuff.

Despite the challenges of A Life Alone, the rewards are great, and I want all of them that may be out there. Plus, I keep growing because I have an end game in mind. No matter the bitterness of today, as I age I find that I'm smoothing out a bit. And, when I grow up, I want to be fine wine.